Miguel Cabrera

By Jon M. Fishman

AMAZING ATHLETES

Lerner Publications Company • Minneapolis

Lerner Publications Company
A division of Lerner Publishing Group, Inc.
241 First Avenue North
Minneapolis, MN 55401 U.S.A.

Website address: www.lernerbooks.com

Library of Congress Cataloging-in-Publication Data

Fishman, Jon M.
    Miguel Cabrera / by Jon M. Fishman.
       p.   cm. — (Amazing athletes)
    Includes index.
    ISBN 978-1-4677-1558-4 (lib. bdg. : alk. paper)
    1. Cabrera, Miguel, 1983—Juvenile literature. 2. Baseball players—Venezuela—Biography—Juvenile literature. 3. Baseball players—United States—Biography—Juvenile literature. I. Title.
GV865.C25F57 2013
796.357092—dc23   2012041771

Manufactured in the United States of America
1 – BP – 12/31/12

Table of Contents

Miguel tries to get a hit against the Kansas City Royals.

BASEBALL'S KING

Detroit Tigers third baseman Miguel Cabrera gripped his bat and stood in the **batter's box**. He lifted his front foot and took a mighty swing at the pitch. Bang! The baseball sailed high into the night sky in Kansas City, Missouri. It cleared the right field fence for a home run.

This 2012 **Major League Baseball (MLB)** game was important for Miguel and the Tigers. They would win the **Central Division** of the **American League (AL)** with a win over the Kansas City Royals. Miguel's blast gave Detroit a 2–0 lead in the 6th inning.

The game was also important for another reason. Miguel's home run was his 44th of the 2012 season. This was the most home runs in the AL. Miguel already led the league in **runs batted in (RBIs)** and **batting average**. If he could keep the lead in all three categories until the end of the season, he would win the **Triple Crown**.

Before Miguel, the last player to win the AL Triple Crown was Carl Yastrzemski. Yastrzemski did it with the Boston Red Sox in 1967.

Miguel is ready at third base.

Winning the Triple Crown is rare. No one had done it in the AL for 45 years. But Miguel is one of the best hitters in baseball. He had a chance to make history. "He's unbelievable," said Tigers general manager Dave Dombrowski. "He's a once-in-a-lifetime player."

The Tigers scored four more runs in the 6th inning to take a 6–0 lead. Kansas City couldn't catch up. Detroit won the game, 6–3. They were AL Central Division champions! The Tigers ran onto the field after the final out. They jumped up and down and cheered. Miguel hugged his teammates and waved to the crowd. "It wasn't easy," said Detroit first baseman Prince Fielder. "But we got it done."

Miguel's teammate Prince Fielder catches a fly ball against the Royals.

The Tigers were headed to the **playoffs**. But Miguel knew that it wasn't yet time to celebrate. He focuses on one game at a time. "We wanted to win this game," he said. "We did it." Miguel knows that winning the World Series is the biggest prize.

Detroit had won the AL Central for the second year in a row. But there were still two games to be played in the 2012 regular season. Miguel led Texas Rangers slugger Josh Hamilton by one home run. Would Miguel be able to hold onto his lead and win the Triple Crown?

Texas outfielder Josh Hamilton had one of his best seasons in 2012.

Miguel was born in the city of Maracay, Venezuela.

FAMILY BUSINESS

Jose Miguel Torres Cabrera was born on April 18, 1983, in Maracay, Venezuela. His family called him Miguel. Venezuela is a country on the northern coast of the continent of South America.

Miguel grew up in a baseball family. His uncle, David Torres, played in the **minor leagues** for the St. Louis Cardinals. Gregoria, Miguel's mother, played 14 seasons as **shortstop** for Venezuela's national softball team. His father, also named Miguel, played pro baseball in Venezuela. Miguel has a younger sister named Ruth.

Miguel has loved baseball for as long as anyone can remember. "It was like he was born with a glove on his hand," said his mother. The Cabreras lived next to a baseball field in the La Pedrera neighborhood of Maracay. Miguel climbed the wall that separated his yard from the field to watch games.

When Miguel wasn't watching a game, he was playing baseball with his father or uncle. It was clear that Miguel had talent. And he had big dreams. "He was 6 or 7 when he told me, 'I want to be a professional baseball player,'" said Miguel's grandmother, Norberta Torres.

Miguel played on a field like this one in Venezuela when he was a child.

Miguel's father loved baseball. But he worried about his son's future. The family didn't have much money. The elder Miguel's baseball career was over. He worked as a car mechanic to provide for his family. He wanted his son to study hard and go to college. "You don't want to be like me," the elder Miguel told his son. Miguel didn't let his father's fears stop him from playing the game he loved. He played as much as he could and got better and better—especially at bat.

Baseball **scouts** began to hear about the young slugger. In 1998, the Florida Marlins (now known as the Miami Marlins) sent scout Louie Eljaua to meet 15-year-old Miguel. Eljaua waited at the field next to Miguel's house. A young man climbed the wall and jumped onto the field. It was Miguel.

Scouts like these look for baseball talent around the world.

Miguel grabbed a bat and stepped up to the plate. "He hit out [of the stadium] eight or nine in a row, and I shut him down," said Eljaua. "We were losing all our balls." The scout told the Marlins that he had found baseball's next big star in Maracay.

Scouts could tell that Miguel had a chance to be a star when he was still just a teenager.

GETTING PAID

The Florida Marlins knew that Miguel had a chance to be a great player. But baseball rules say that players cannot sign a **contract** with a team until they are 16 years old. The Marlins would have to wait eight months before offering Miguel a contract.

Miguel continued to grow and play baseball. The Marlins stayed in touch with him and his family. By 1999, Miguel was 6 feet 2 inches tall and weighed 190 pounds. He turned 16 in April and could sign a contract with the Marlins. But other MLB teams had heard about the big basher from Maracay. Teams such as the New York Yankees and the Los Angeles Dodgers also wanted Miguel. They offered him millions of dollars to sign a contract.

The Marlins won the World Series in 1997.

Alex Gonzalez makes a hard throw to first base.

Miguel decided to sign with the Marlins. The team had worked hard to build a bond with Miguel and his family. Florida was a good team. They had won the World Series in 1997. And the Marlins' shortstop was Alex Gonzalez. Gonzalez was also from Venezuela and one of Miguel's favorite players. Florida gave Miguel $1.8 million. He was rich!

Miguel began his pro baseball career in 2000 with the Gulf Coast League (GCL) Marlins. This is the Florida Marlins' lowest minor-league team. Miguel was only 17 years old. Most of the other players in the GCL were older.

Miguel hit only two home runs in 65 games in the GCL. It would take some time before he'd be ready for the major leagues. In 2001, Miguel played for the Class A Kane County Cougars. He hit seven home runs in 110 games.

Miguel bats during a Cougars game.

There was big news for Miguel off the field in 2002. He married his high school sweetheart, Rosangel, in a ceremony in Maracay.

Miguel moved up to the Class A-Advanced Jupiter Hammerheads in 2002. He hit nine home runs in 124 games. He also had 43 **doubles**. Many scouts thought some of those doubles would become home runs as Miguel got older and stronger.

Mike Lowell makes a throw from third base.

THE BIG SHOW

The Marlins knew that Miguel was on a fast track to the major leagues. He was big and strong. He crushed the ball to all directions of the field. It wouldn't be long before the hard-hitting third baseman would be ready for baseball's biggest stage. But the Marlins already had a good third baseman. Mike Lowell was on his way to his best season as a pro in 2003.

Miguel's fourth season of pro baseball began with the Class AA Carolina Mudcats. The team decided to move Miguel to the outfield. It would be easier to find playing time for him in the outfield when he proved ready to move up to the major leagues.

Miguel crushed the ball again and again during the 2003 season. He hit 10 home runs in just 65 games with the Mudcats. His .365 batting average was one of the best on the team. At the same time, the Marlins' left fielder was struggling. Todd Hollandsworth hit only three home runs with a .254 batting average in 2003.

Miguel was called up to the major leagues and took Hollandsworth's spot in left field. His

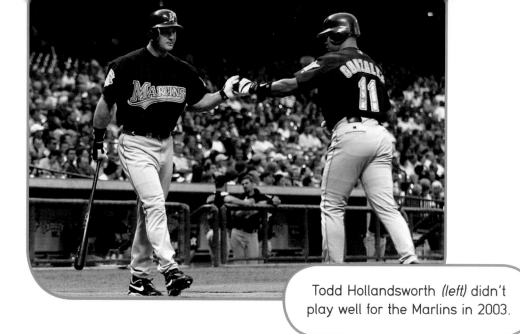

Todd Hollandsworth *(left)* didn't play well for the Marlins in 2003.

first game with the Marlins was on June 20, 2003. The Marlins faced the Tampa Bay Devil Rays (now known as the Tampa Bay Rays).

The game didn't start out well for Miguel. He struck out in his first at bat. In his next at bat, he hit into a **double play**. In the ninth inning, Miguel made another easy out. But the game was tied and went into extra innings. Miguel had another chance in the 11th. This time, he made the most of it. Miguel hit a long home run to centerfield to win the game.

Miguel gets ready to make a catch.

Miguel's father had been watching from Maracay. But he fell asleep before the game ended. He went to the store the next day to get a newspaper. When he read that Miguel had ended the game with a home run, he shouted for joy. "I told the clerk that I wanted to buy all the papers," Miguel's father said. "He thought I was nuts."

The Marlins ended the 2003 season with a record of 91–71. They were headed to the playoffs. They took down the San Francisco Giants in the first round. Then they knocked out the Chicago Cubs. The Marlins were headed to the World Series in Miguel's first season!

Miguel jogs around the bases after hitting a home run.

BASEBALL'S BIGGEST STAR

Miguel and the Marlins faced the New York Yankees in the 2003 World Series. The Yankees had already won the World Series 26 times. Most people expected them to beat the Marlins and become world champions for the 27th time.

New York won two of the first three games. The Yankees sent Roger Clemens to the **pitcher's mound** for Game 4. Clemens is one of the best pitchers in baseball history.

Miguel stepped to the plate in the first inning with a runner on base. Clemens threw his first pitch at 92 miles per hour. The ball raced toward Miguel and sailed just beneath his chin. Miguel bent back to avoid getting hit by the ball. He stared out at Clemens before digging in for the next pitch. A few pitches later, Clemens threw the ball high and away from Miguel. But the big third baseman leaned across the plate and crushed

Roger Clemens had a long baseball career. Miguel had just turned one year old when Clemens pitched in his first major-league game in 1984.

Miguel (wearing number 20) celebrates winning the World Series with his teammates.

the ball. It sailed deep into right field for a home run. The Marlins had the lead, 2–0.

The Yankees came back to tie the game. But Florida won in the 12th inning when Miguel's friend Alex Gonzalez smashed a home run. Miguel and the Marlins took the next two games to win the World Series!

Miguel was a World Series winner. He averaged more than 31 home runs and 115 RBIs over his next four seasons with the Marlins. But he hadn't forgotten his friends and family in Maracay. "He grew up in a poor neighborhood," said Victor Celis, a fan of Miguel's in Venezuela. "He played in the World Series and came home and is still the same person."

The Marlins decided that they needed to make changes to their team in 2007. They traded Miguel to the Detroit Tigers for several **prospects**. Miguel hit at least 30 home runs and 103 RBIs over his next five seasons. But his best year came in 2012. With only two games to go, Miguel led the AL with 44 home runs, 137 RBIs, and a .329 batting average. No one could catch him. Miguel won the Triple Crown.

"It was hard the last two days because everybody talked about [the Triple Crown]," said Miguel. "I just had to focus." Tigers manager Jim Leyland knew Miguel could do it. "I've managed a lot of players, and some great ones, but I've never seen anything like this," Leyland said.

Miguel signs autographs for fans.

Miguel makes a diving catch during Game 1 of the 2012 World Series.

The Tigers headed to the playoffs. They beat the Oakland Athletics and the Yankees to reach the World Series! But Detroit lost to the San Francisco Giants in four games.

Miguel has become one of baseball's greatest players. He still loves the game as much as he did as a child. "I always like to play," said Miguel after winning the Triple Crown. "You're going to see me [on the field], having fun and playing hard to win games."

Selected Career Highlights

2012   Won the AL Triple Crown
Named to All-Star Game for the seventh time

2011   Named to the All-Star Game for the sixth time
Won the AL batting title for the first time

2010   Named to the All-Star Game for the fifth time
Won the Silver Slugger award as best-hitting first
baseman in the AL
Finished second in the AL batting title race

2009   Finished fourth in the AL batting title race

2008   Traded to the Detroit Tigers
Finished first in the AL in home runs

2007   Named to the All-Star Game for the fourth
time

2006   Named to the All-Star Game for the third time
Won Silver Slugger award as the best-hitting third
baseman in the National League (NL)
Finished second in the NL batting title race

2005   Named to the All-Star Game for the second time
Won the Silver Slugger award as one of the three best-hitting
outfielders in the NL
Finished third in the NL batting title race

2004   Named to the All-Star Game for the first time

2003   Played in his first MLB game with the Florida Marlins

2002   Played for the Class A-Advanced Jupiter Hammerheads

2001   Played for the Class A Kane County Cougars

2000   Played his first pro season in the GCL

1999   Signed his first contract with the Florida Marlins

Glossary

American League (AL): one of MLB's two leagues. The AL has 15 teams, including the Detroit Tigers, the Kansas City Royals, the Texas Rangers, and the New York Yankees.

batter's box: the areas on each side of home plate where batters stand

batting average: a number that describes how often a baseball player gets a hit

Central Division: one of the three groups of teams that make up the AL. The AL Central is made up of the Chicago White Sox, the Cleveland Indians, the Detroit Tigers, the Kansas City Royals, and the Minnesota Twins.

contract: a written deal between a player and a team or a company

double play: a play in which two outs are made

doubles: hits that allow batters to safely reach second base

Major League Baseball (MLB): the top group of professional men's baseball teams in North America. MLB is divided into the American League and the National League.

minor leagues: a group of teams where players work to improve their skills in hopes of moving up to the major leagues

pitcher's mound: the hill in the center of the baseball diamond where the pitcher stands when pitching

playoffs: a series of games played after the regular season to determine a champion

prospects: players whom scouts believe will someday be good major-league players

runs batted in (RBIs): the number of runners able to score on a batter's hit or walk

scouts: people who judge the skills of players

shortstop: a player who plays in the field between second and third base

Triple Crown: an award in baseball for a player who leads his league in batting average, home runs, and RBIs

Further Reading & Websites

Jones, Helga. *Venezuela*. Minneapolis: Lerner Publications Company, 2008.

Kennedy, Mike, and Mark Stewart. *Long Ball: The Legend and Lore of the Home Run*. Minneapolis: Millbrook Press, 2006.

Savage, Jeff. *Josh Hamilton*. Minneapolis: Lerner Publications Company, 2009.

Savage, Jeff. *Justin Verlander*. Minneapolis: Lerner Publications Company, 2013.

Savage, Jeff. *Prince Fielder*. Minneapolis: Lerner Publications Company, 2013.

Detroit Tigers: The Official Site
http://www.detroit.tigers.mlb.com
The official website of the Detroit Tigers includes the team schedule and game results, biographies of Miguel Cabrera and other players and coaches, and much more.

Major League Baseball: The Official Site
http://www.mlb.com
The official Major League Baseball website provides fans with game results, statistics, schedules, and biographies of all players.

Sports Illustrated Kids
http://www.sikids.com
The *Sports Illustrated Kids* website covers all sports, including baseball.

Index

Photo Acknowledgments

The images in this book are used with the permission of: © John Sleezer/ Kansas City Star/MCT via Getty Images, p. 4; © Jeff Moffett/Icon SMI, p. 6; AP Photo/Charlie Riedel, p. 7; © Rick Yeatts/Getty Images, p. 8; © R. S. Daniell/ Art Directors & TRIP, p. 9; AP Photo/Ariana Cubillos, p. 11; © Matt May/US Presswire, p. 13; AP Photo/Tony Gutierrez, p. 14; AP Photo/Eric Draper, p. 15; AP Photo/Alan Diaz, p. 16; © Todd Rosenberg/Sports Illustrated/Getty Images, p. 17; © Eliot J. Schechter/Getty Images, pp. 19, 22; © James Nielsen/ AFP/Getty Images, p. 21; © Linda Cataffo/NY Daily News Archive via Getty Images, p. 23; © Corey Sipkin/NY Daily News Archive via Getty Images, p 25; © Leon Halip/Getty Images, p. 27; © Thearon W. Henderston/Getty Images, p. 28; © Steven King/Icon SMI, p. 29.

Front cover: © Mark Cunningham/MLB Photos via Getty Images.

Main body text set in Caecilia LT Std 55 Roman 16/28.
Typeface provided by Adobe Systems.